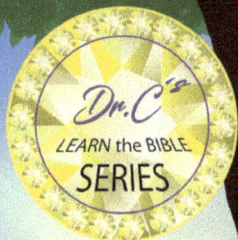

E IS FOR
EVE

Dr. C. White-Elliott
Illustrated by Ariel

www.clfpublishing.org
909.315.3161

Illustrations by Ariel.

ISBN # 978-1-945102-52-3

Printed in the United States of America.

For

Kimara Tsehai Faith White

my granddaughter

God had formed Adam from the dust of the

ground and placed him in the garden called

Eden. Adam's job was to name all the animals.

After Adam had named the animals, God saw

"no suitable helper was found for Adam"

(Genesis 2:20). God caused Adam to go into a

deep sleep (Genesis 2:21).

While Adam was asleep, God

took out one of his ribs

(Genesis 2:21).

From the rib, God created a woman

and took her to the man.

Later, while Adam and Eve were in the

garden, Eve had a conversation with the

serpent.

After speaking with the serpent, Eve ate

from the tree of the knowledge of good

and evil and shared the fruit with Adam.

God had told Adam before Eve was

created to not eat from that one tree.

Because they were disobedient to God,

they were sent out of the garden.

Later, Eve gave birth to a son named

Cain and a little later to a second son

named Abel. Those were the first two

children born on earth.

Adam, his wife Eve, and their two sons,

Cain and Abel, made up the first family

on earth. Later, Adam and Eve had

other children.